GENDER TREASON

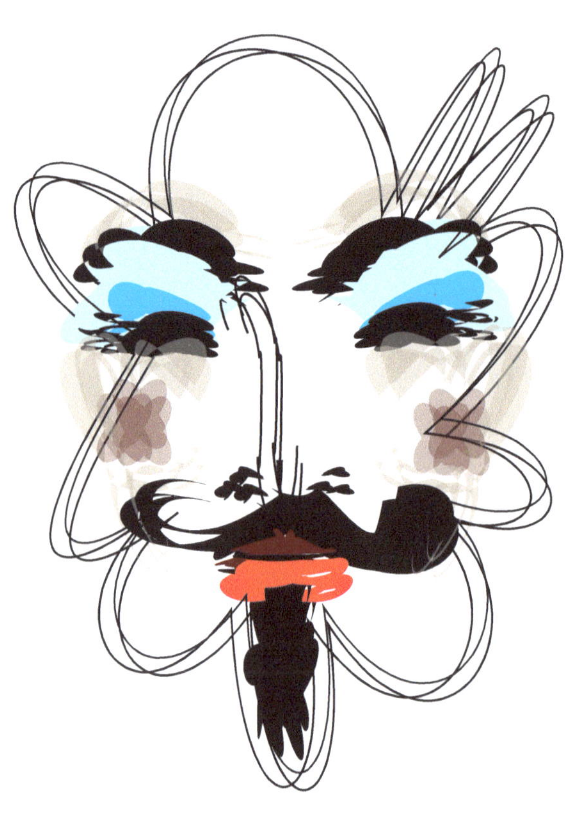

GENDER TREASON

PAINTINGS AND INTERVIEWS BY

RYAN WILKS

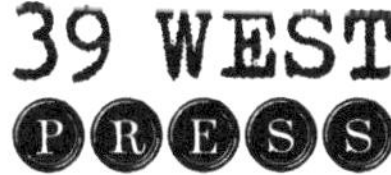

39 WEST PRESS

39 WEST PRESS
Kansas City, MO
www.39WestPress.com

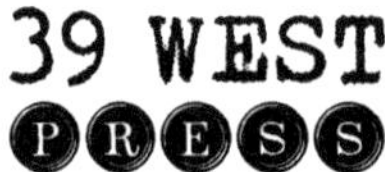

First Edition: July 2016

ISBN: 978-0-9908649-4-3

10 9 8 7 6 5 4 3 2

Paintings & Interviews: Ryan Wilks
Design, Layout, Edits: Ryan Wilks, Jen Harris, Jeanette Powers, j.d.tulloch

39WP-11

Contents

INTRODUCTION

Gender Treason is a series of portrait paintings that chronicles my latest exhibition, which debuted at Leedy-Voulkos Art Center on July 1, 2016, and includes interviews with my subjects, providing a rare glimpse into the lives of queer people living in the Midwest. In an effort to transcend sensationalized media stereotypes and portray a more honest perspective into queer existence, I spent a year interviewing, and then painting, queer Kansas City residents.

The series, which focuses on twelve people who span the queer spectrum of gender and sexual identity, offers a vulnerable insight into each individual's life, their common struggles, and the victories that bond them in a shared human condition. Each painting aspires to capture the complexity and truth of its subject by employing bold colors, painterly brush strokes, and hard lines.

Since the Stonewall riots of 1969 sparked the fight for queer liberation, LGBTQIA equality has breached the mainstream, leading to a national conversation that has helped change the minds of many once bigoted people and contributed to positive legislative changes. But equality is just the start. For true compassion to wrap itself around an entire nation and sustain lasting social growth, education on queer realities by queer people must be encouraged. *Gender Treason* strives to be that brand of education.

I would like to thank the vast number of people, organizations, and publications who have witnessed from start to finish the evolution of *Gender Treason*. If not for the unparalleled support of the Kansas City community, who in various ways funded and encouraged this project, none of this would have been possible; my best friend, Poet Jen Harris, whose voice echoed in me louder than my own fears; my curator Ashley Anders; and the subjects who shared with me their truths, their bodies, and their collective faith in the power of art.

This book is dedicated to any and all people who have ever braved the journey of self ... and to those who are just beginning.

— Ryan Wilks

ANA

What's really weird is I'm an ethnic minority [and] a lesbian woman, but I always felt guilty about the privilege I was given. I've never had a lot of Latino friends. I always struggled with that identity aspect. It's innately ingrained in all minorities that white is better. I also went through a lot of gender identity things: dressed like a skater boy, shaved my head. I thought that's what being gay was. Now, I dress how I want, and I like my long hair. I started embracing my Latina side. I wear Guatemalan clothes a lot, and I love it. I bound my chest one time, but it just wasn't for me. I was exploring my masculine side. I just didn't know how to be gay. It comes with gender. And in relationships, you kind of want to go into heteronormative roles, but it's not my thing. It never really was. I tried to be butch or femme, soft butch: all these labels that just don't apply to me. I want to be able to express myself in a way that's true to myself and is balanced and doesn't feel contrived. I tell people to love themselves. Embrace who you are.

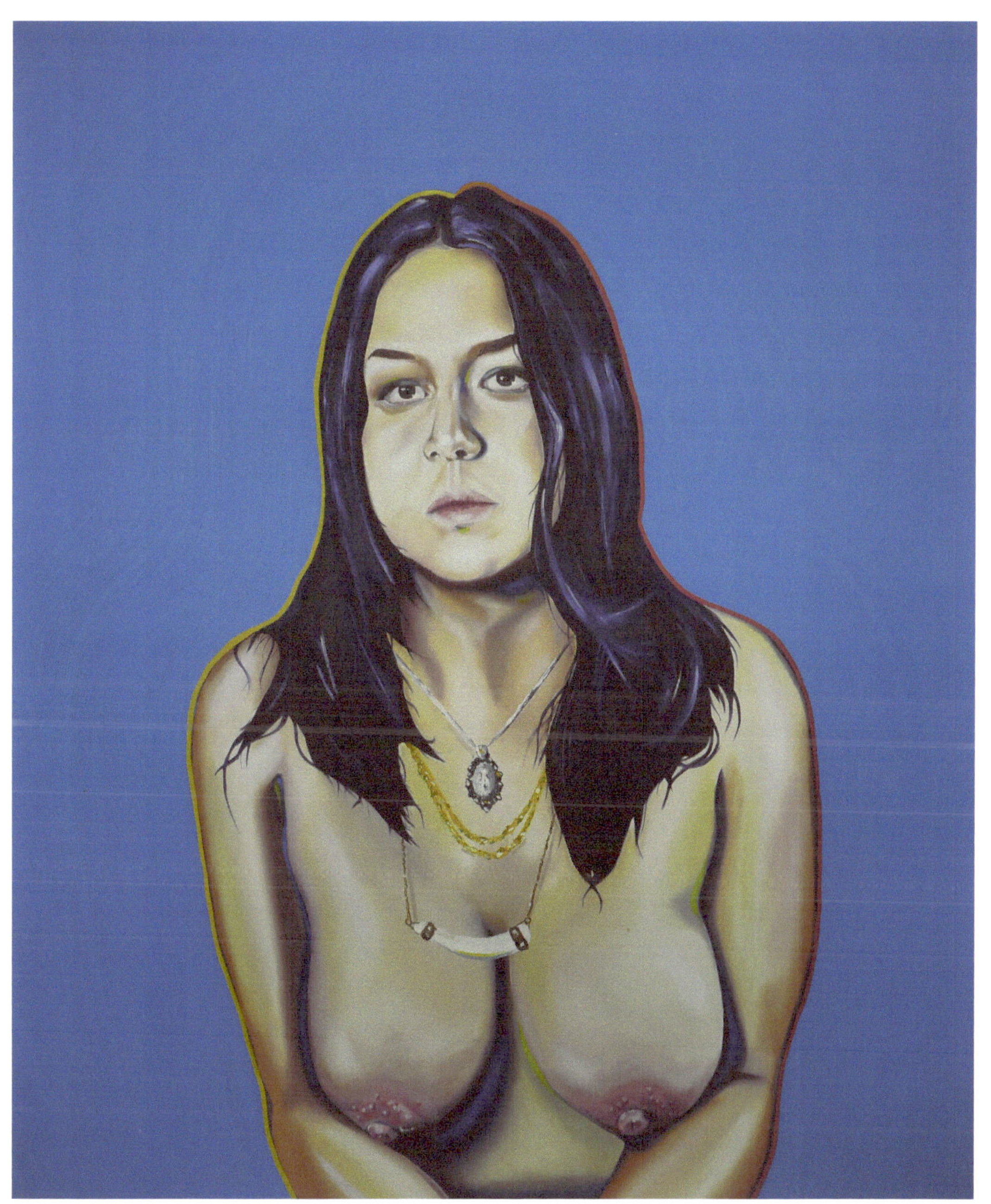

ANDY

There was more than Stonewall. Know your history. Know the people who came before. Know the people who have allowed you to go forward. I don't feel treasonous to my gender; the male peacock is the prettiest bird of the two. Men have worn makeup and loved luxury and beautiful fabrics and beautiful tailoring for years, for-EVER ... and all of a sudden it became synonymous with being gay ... and then all of a sudden, men couldn't love beautiful details and pleats and ruffles and lace. I was just thinking ... *Gender Treason* seems weird to me in that context. It's nothing new. It's not a modern invention. It's not a trend. You are part of a tribe and a group of people that are millions of years old. You have to look at the bigger picture. You're not alone.

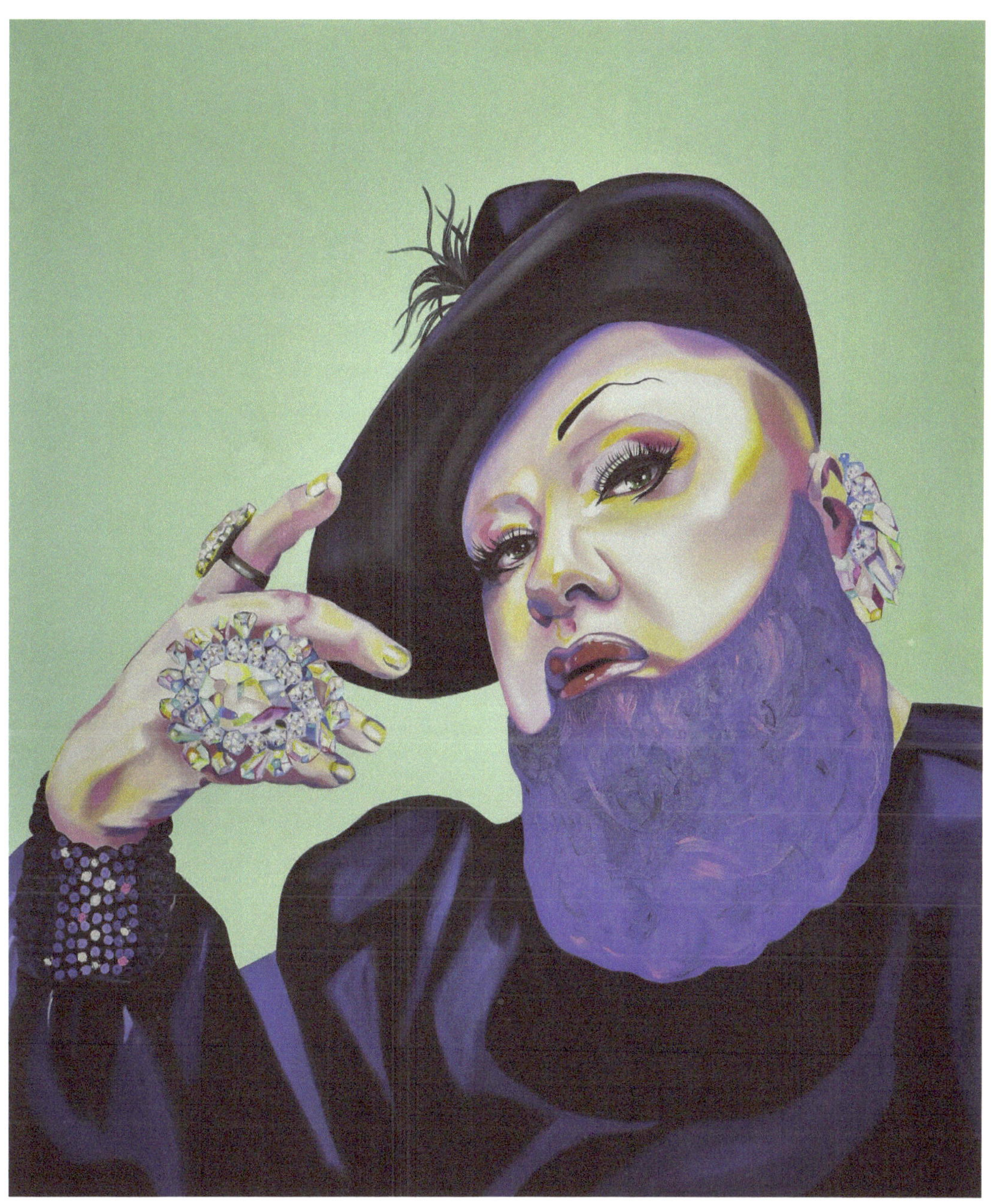

Anonymous

Telling people, "disclosing" as they call it, has been a challenge. It's already an uphill battle: being a gay man, choosing a nonconventional career path, and things along those lines. I don't need to add anything more to that as far as public knowledge. This is just a problem. It's like being half-blind, maybe, or having asthma. It's just another item on my to-do list once a month. I view it as an injustice. I don't want to speak for anyone else in the project, but almost everyone is being represented in some aspect of their identity. Being [queer] is part of their personality, part of their vibrancy, their wavelength. Their connection to the worldly creative process is integrated in that, but it comes with its share of injustices because of the society we live in. Being [HIV] positive is, in itself, an injustice. I guess some people get past feeling judged about it or having a feeling of shame about it. I'm not sure that I will. That might be the least curable aspect of the condition. I plan on outliving everyone I know and taking it to the grave with me.

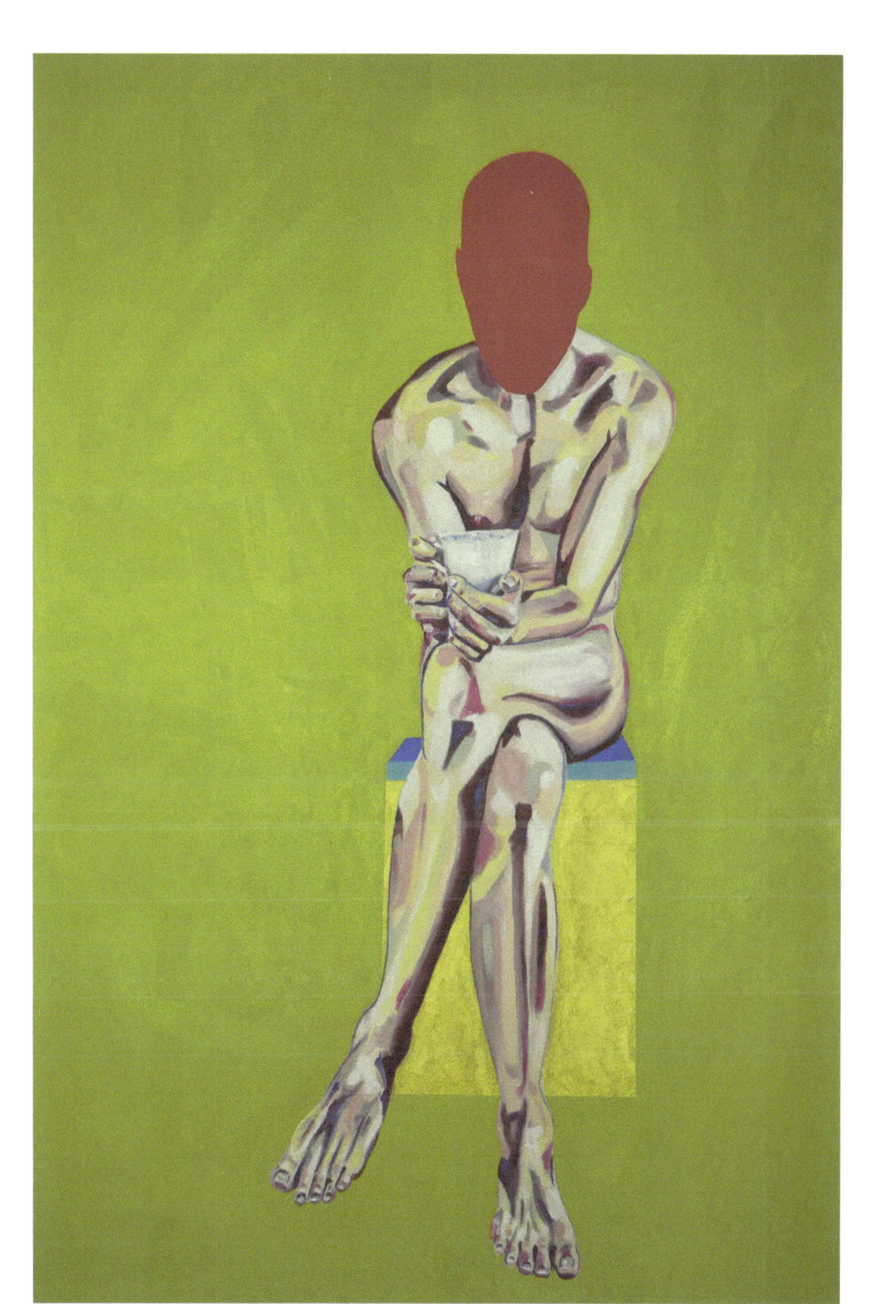

Avery

I think society gives us examples, whether it's in TV shows or things you don't register as seeing. There are things that are acceptable and things that are not, and you learn very quickly that you are one of the things that are not. If you ask me to describe myself to you, being gay might come in on the second page. There are so many other descriptors and so many other things about myself that I would tell you about—about who I was—that in all likelihood, I might forget to say that I was gay … not out of a desire to hide, but it is not the primary focus of my life, or my personality, or my interests. It's not the primary aspect of my identity. Filmmaker, entrepreneur, artist, writer, speaker, spiritual … all these things would come before the word "gay" ever left my lips.

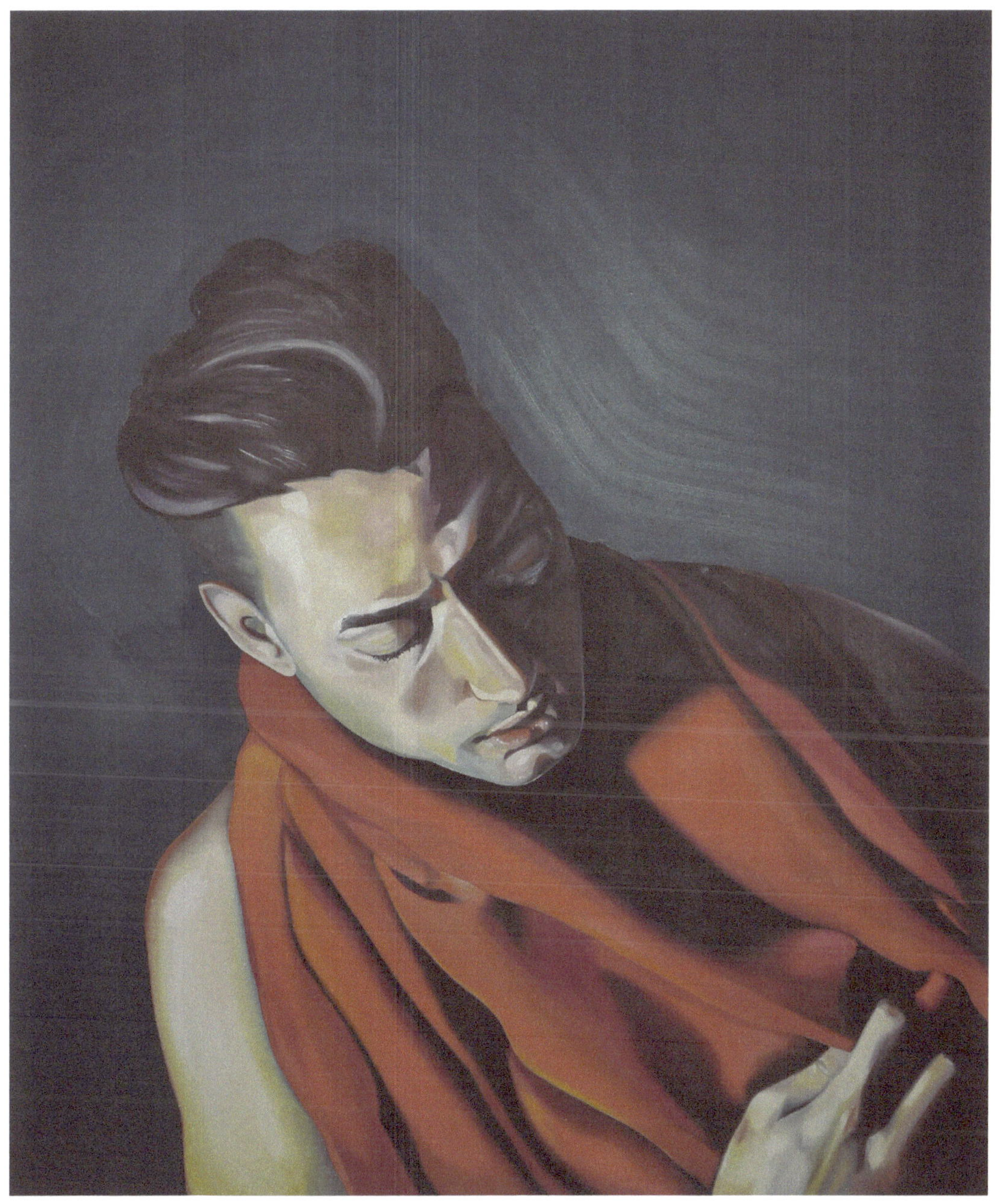

Brian

When you "sound gay" as a kid, they try to correct it. It wasn't totally obvious what they were doing, but when I realized someone was trying to correct something about me, I would try to hide that something rather than being who I am. Gay men butch or femme it up. There's a whole interesting aspect of it, being who other people expect you to be or want you to be. I feel like I change myself for people quite often. A big, transitional part of my life has been getting out of the relationship I've been in for the last two years. I have this body image stuff and am conscious of it and the way I look and trying to accept that THAT is me ... the intersection of that. I felt pressured to be vegan when I was dating a vegan. I felt pressure in my last relationship to be who he wanted me to be or not be who he didn't want me to be. Getting out of that relationship is making me realize who I am or making me realize how well I don't know myself and what it means to find that.

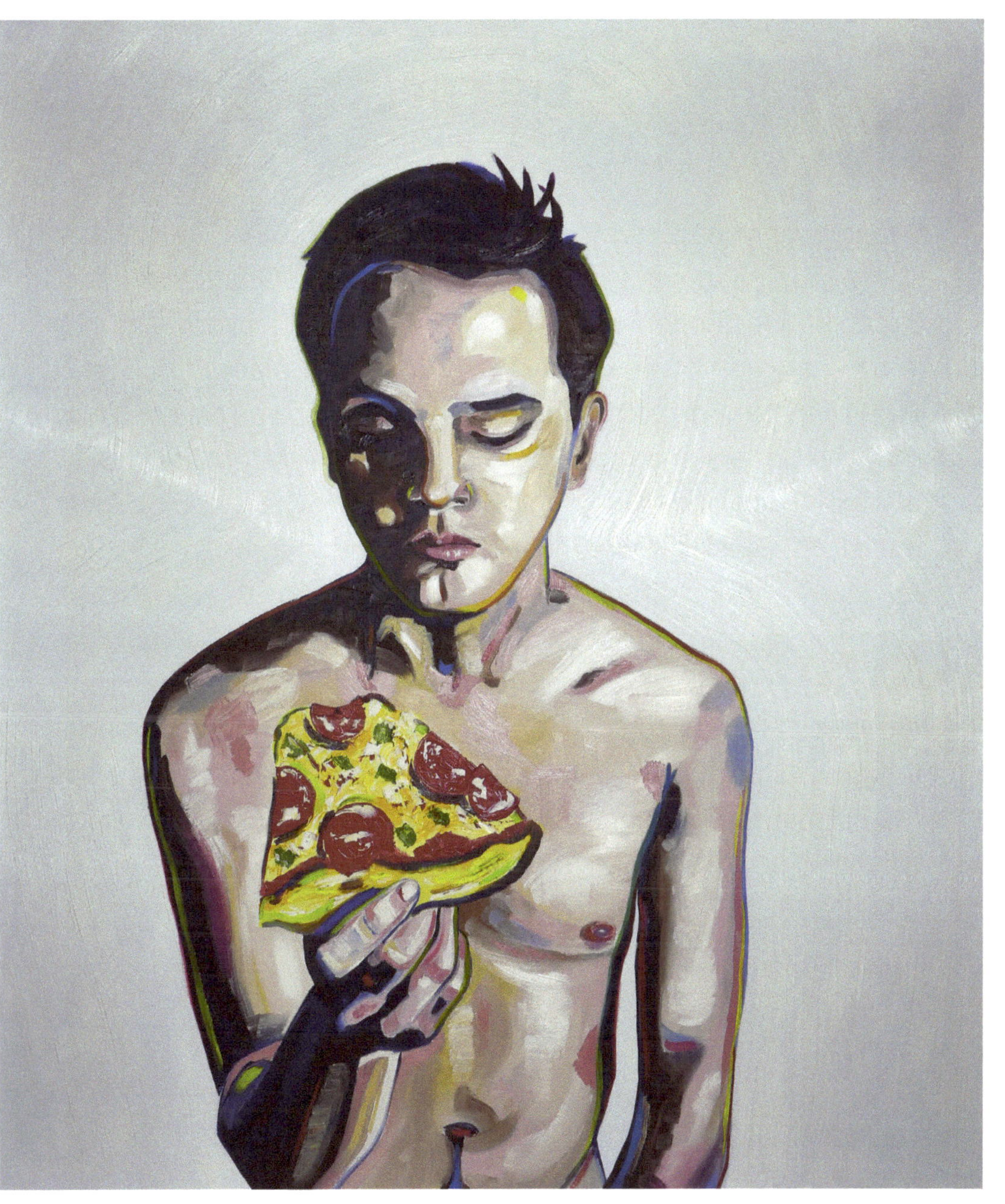

EUGENE

When I was younger, my dialect was way different. I remember being young and being with my mom, and she would talk to us. But then her phone would ring and she would pick up, and her voice changed. It was mainly with banks and places like that. I asked her, "Why do you change your voice?" And she said, "So that they can understand me." There are all these stereotypes about black gay men, and I think I don't really fit into what people expect out of me, especially when I open my mouth. I think they expect me to even sound different; they don't expect me to articulate as I do. If you want people to understand things, you have to meet them where they are. What I'm coming to find is what's normal for me isn't normal for everyone else, and what I want my normal to be is me being in love with a man and happy. That's all I want my normal to be. I don't care what color that person is. I can't control what color I am. That's what normal is for me.

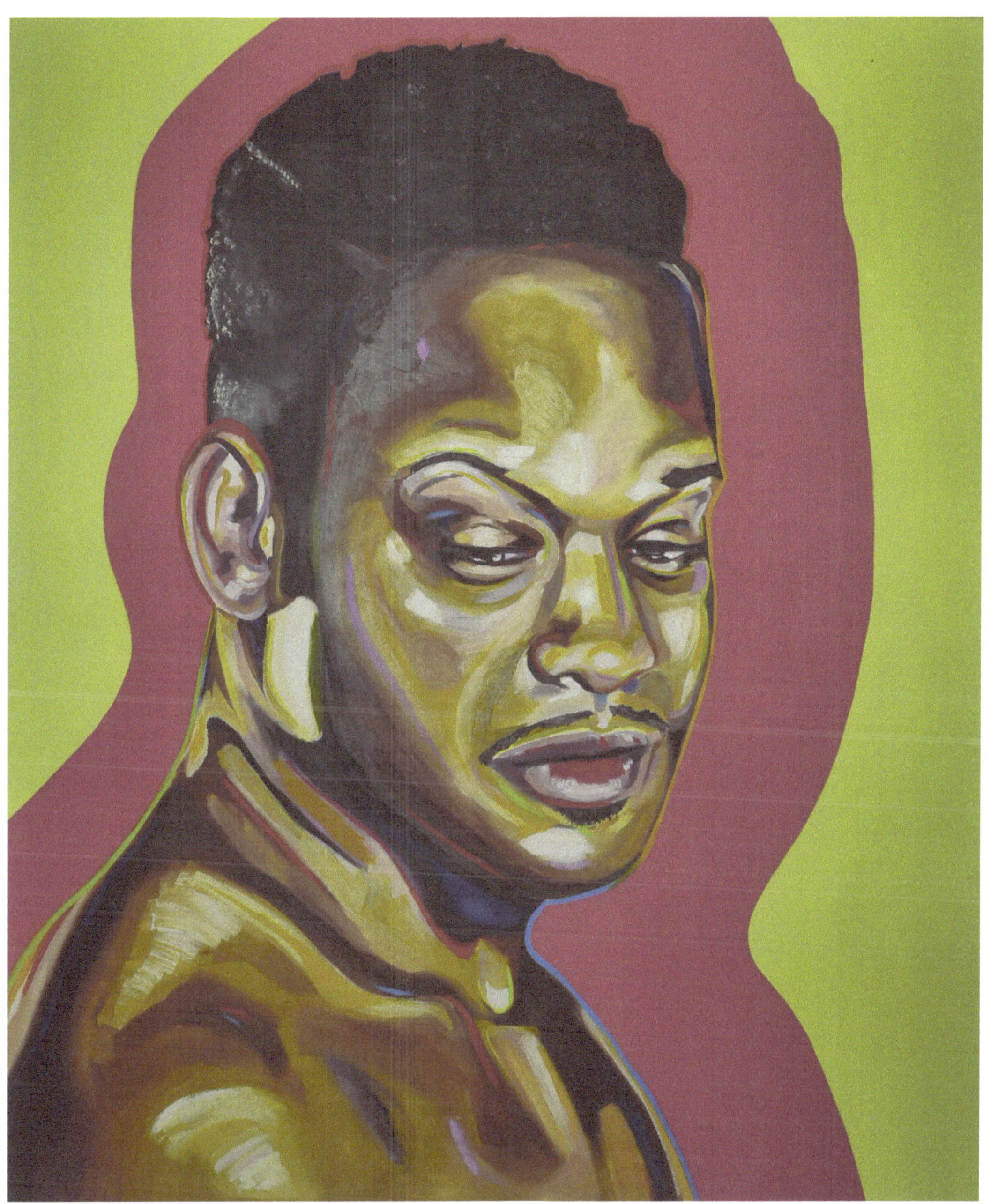

GRANT

I've always been really into painting, and that transferred into makeup artistry because it's painting on your face. I really want to show that makeup is art. I want to do everything. I want to be a photographer, fashion designer, make-up artist, drag queen, maybe a performer. I want to bring my art to world. I want to bring androgyny to the world. I think it's important in this day and age to recognize that we don't have to label everything … that I can just be Grant. Coming out was really easy. My mom was super accepting, and she basically knew that I was gay. I think I was ten years old. I was in 5th or 6th grade. I'm my most authentic self, living as a queer person and being gay. It's kind of affected my life, because [I'm homeschooled], and I'm just now having gay teenage friends. And I've kind of learned of all of the drama and drugs and smoking and alcohol that I wasn't really aware of. I guess I was kind of naïve about seeing that people can crumble under pressure or under a family that doesn't accept them.

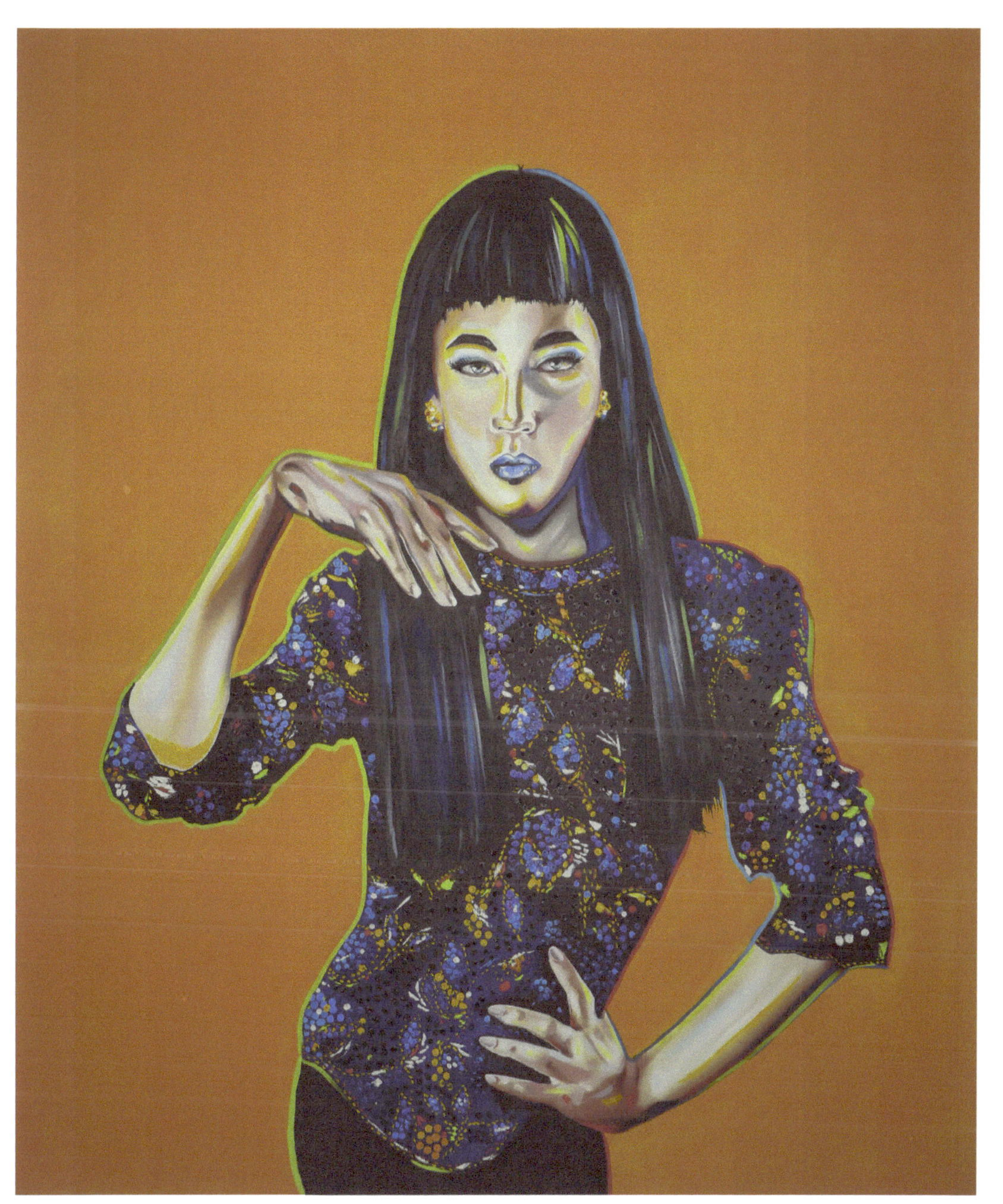

IVORY

Who I am is a very long story. I was adopted at the age of six or seven. I don't consider myself a son. I don't consider myself a daughter. I consider myself, Me. I ran away when I was fifteen. The last thing my mom ever told me was she'd wished she adopted my brother instead of me. Ever since I was a kid, I always felt like … I just wasn't. That's it. I didn't know what I wasn't, and I didn't know what I was. I felt like maybe I wanted to be something else, but it wasn't to the point that I was ashamed of who I was: other people were. They looked at me like I wasn't exactly right. My whole process of finding myself was very gradual. I just found myself a few years ago: I transitioned. I wanted to see if male to female would work for me, and I feel like inside that I am [female]. But my outside isn't really congruent with that. There's no gender to be congruent with. "Non-binary" is the best word I can use to describe my gender. I think I'm neither male nor female. I'm just me.

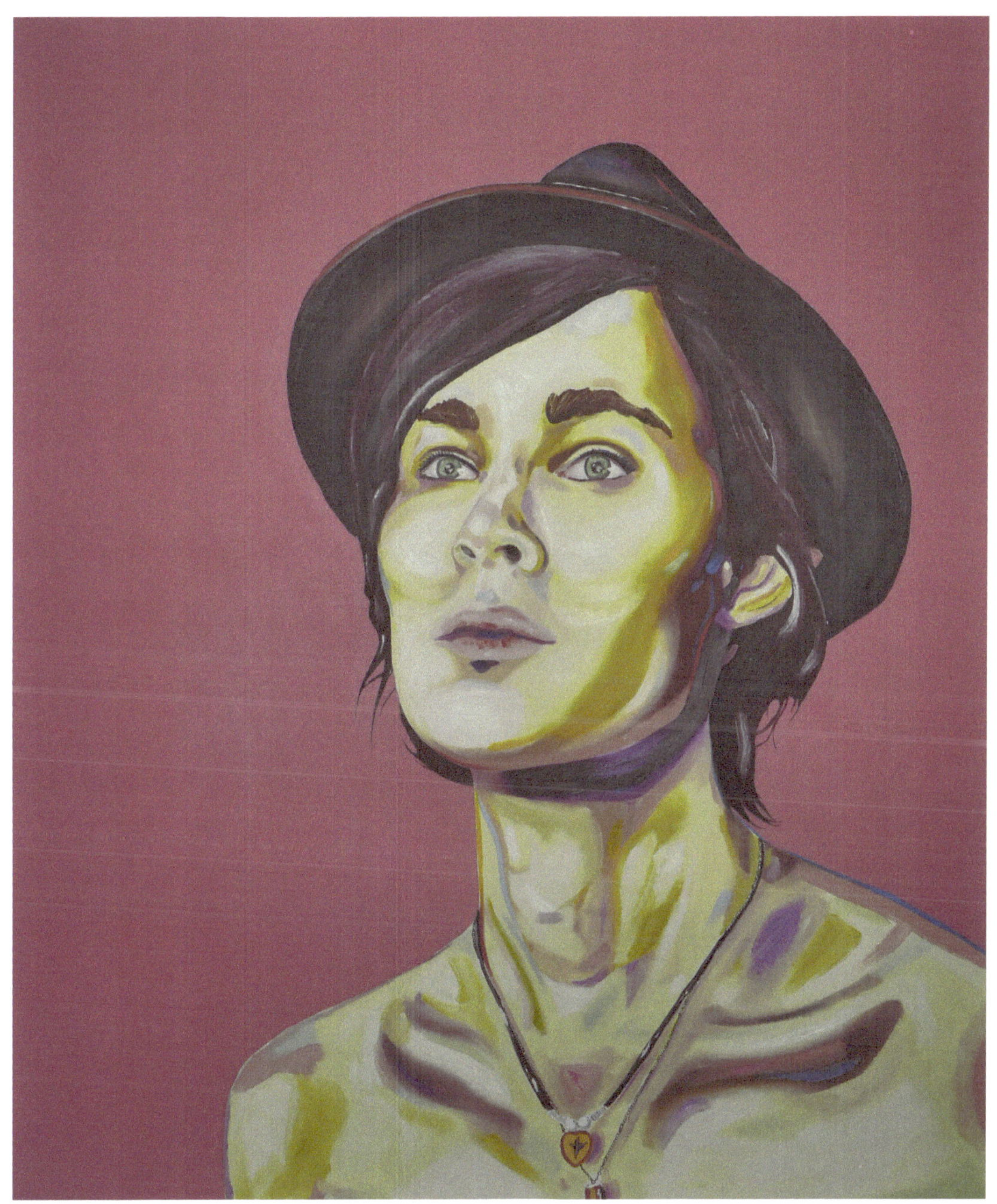

Madeline

I spent years fighting it: so much energy that goes into trying to hide yourself. It's an exhausting way to live. You have no energy for anything else because you're so busy trying to bottle up who you are and pretend you're not who you are for the world because you think the world is going to hate you. When you reach that place of finally not caring what the world thinks, but also where you just know you can no longer not be yourself, you have to let it out and let it be or else die. Then, that's such a great place of freedom. It was a prison before. Now, it's liberation. It's freedom. It's truly living my real self. Of course there are still challenges every day with old habits because you don't just change who you were overnight. You don't just let go of everything and all of a sudden everything's brand new again. There's still old habits to break, old thought patterns to release. However, coming from a fresh point, a point of authenticity, it's just … it's amazing. It's just so … I feel freedom.

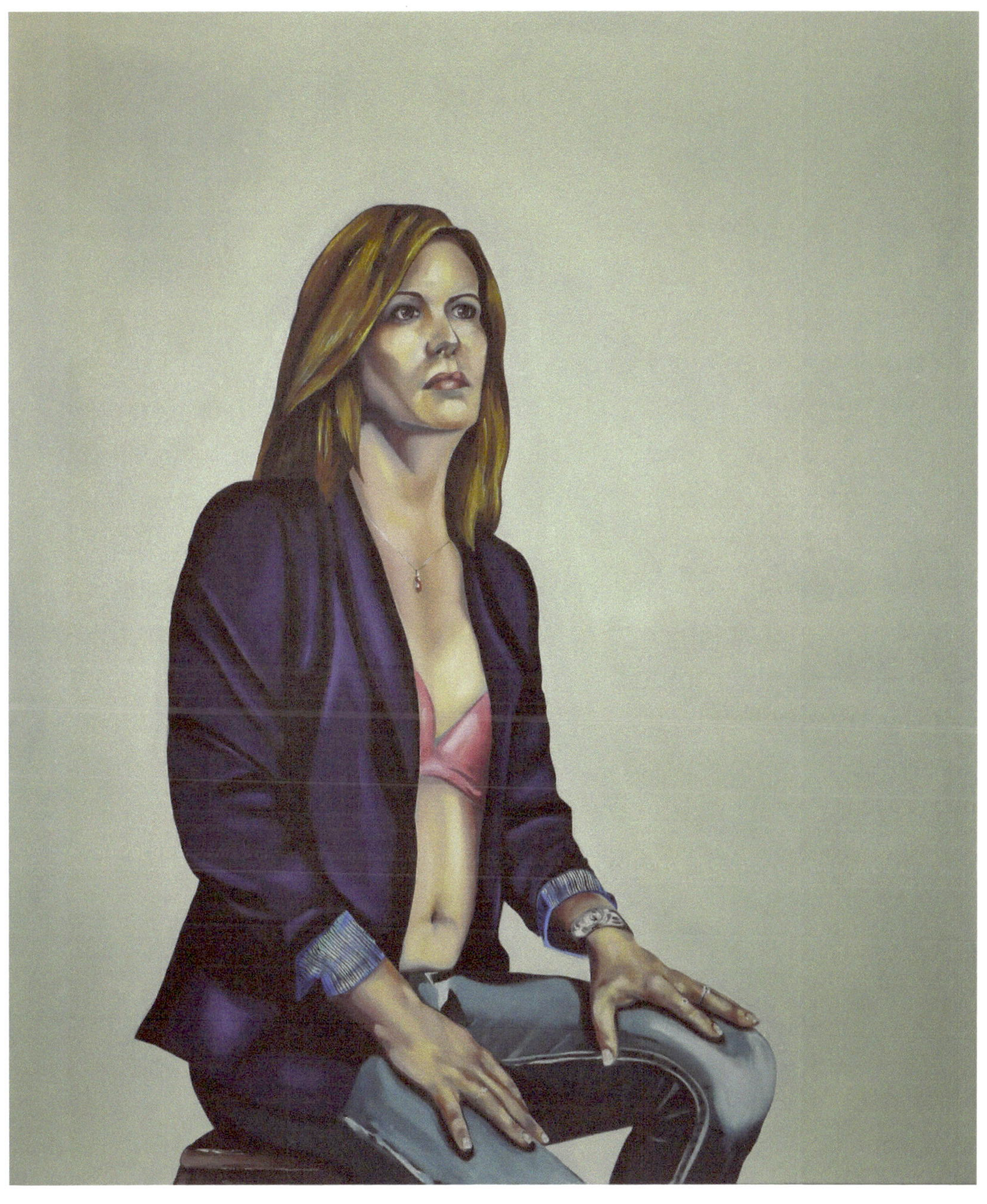

MELISSA

My parents didn't know [I was gay], and my mom didn't take it well at all. She basically disowned me. She told my kids I was going to burn in hell, that I wasn't gonna go to heaven. So my kids would come to me and say, "We don't want you to die. Can you not be a lesbian anymore?" I think the culture of black people in church is huge. Church is all we knew. That stems from all the way back to slavery, when that's all we had. That's everything to us. When we're sad, when we're depressed, we go to church. We don't go see a psychologist; we go to church. When we need something, we go to the church. The church is everything in the black community, so I think that had a lot to do with it. My thing is always to never victimize someone who doesn't victimize themselves. Yeah, I carry a lot of cultural and historical oppressions, but do I consider myself a victim? Not necessarily. Not as much as I consider myself a survivor.

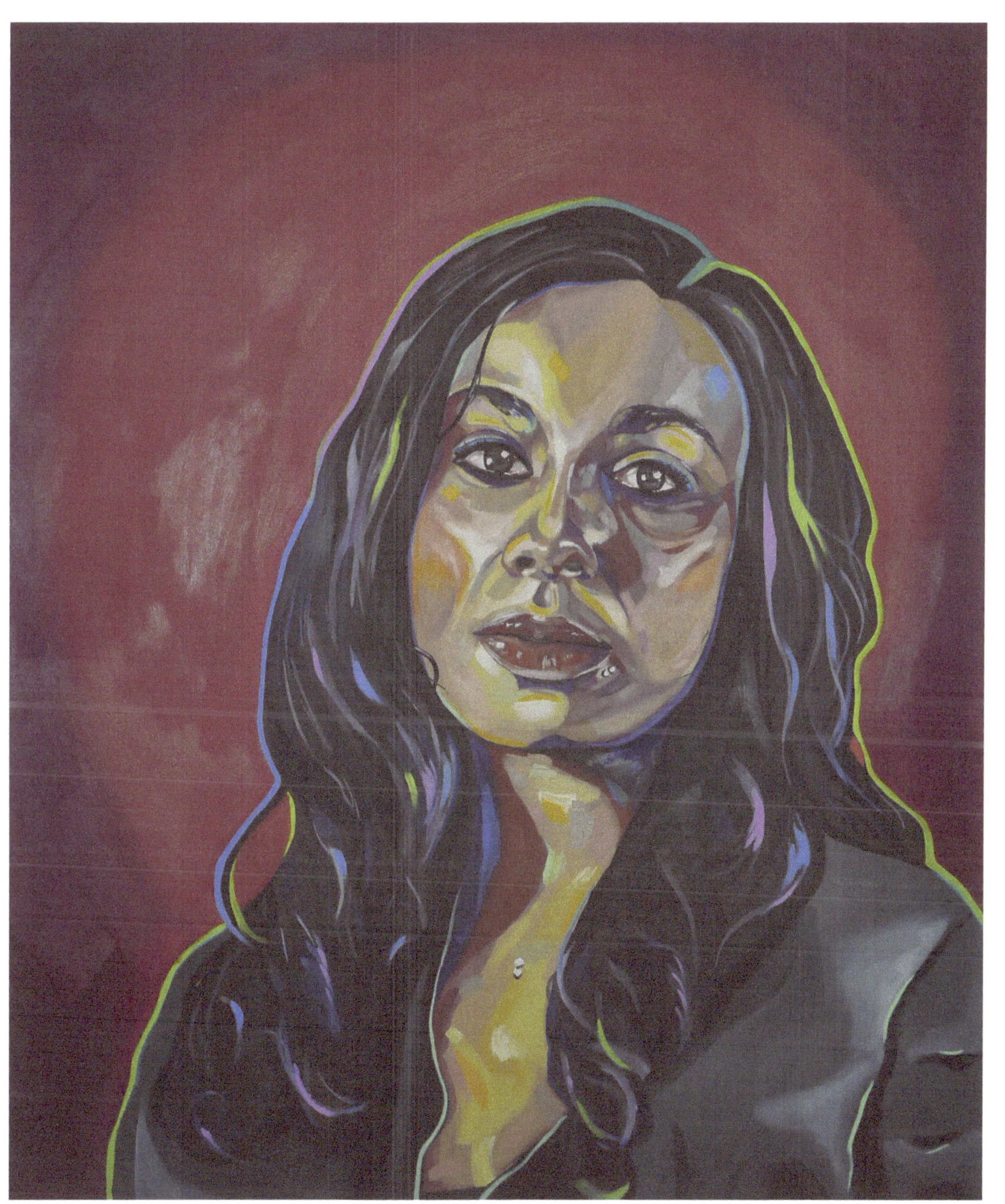

Teddy

Because of living in a world that constantly negates your identity in most any way, you live under a constant state of suspicion about those around you and what people's intentions are. I've run into, personally, a couple of times with gender queer or other trans people having to constantly validate ourselves: "How trans are you?" In medically transitioning, you begin to really butt heads with systems that make you have to prove your identity as a diagnosis. When I was first seeing my therapist, I knew what I had to say to her, which is basically a very standardized trans-narrative which makes you say, "I was born into the wrong body." How dysphoric are you? Tell me how sad and how much you hate yourself ... how much you hate your body. Everyone wants to hear the story of the origin of your self-hatred. I got to see the letter for my diagnosis: diagnosed as "gender dysphoria." You get to see yourself classified in the medical system, and then your diagnosis grants you access to other things. From that point on, transition, medically, becomes a lot of numbers, timetable[s], monetary [numbers], numbers of milligrams of testosterone you're shooting into yourself.

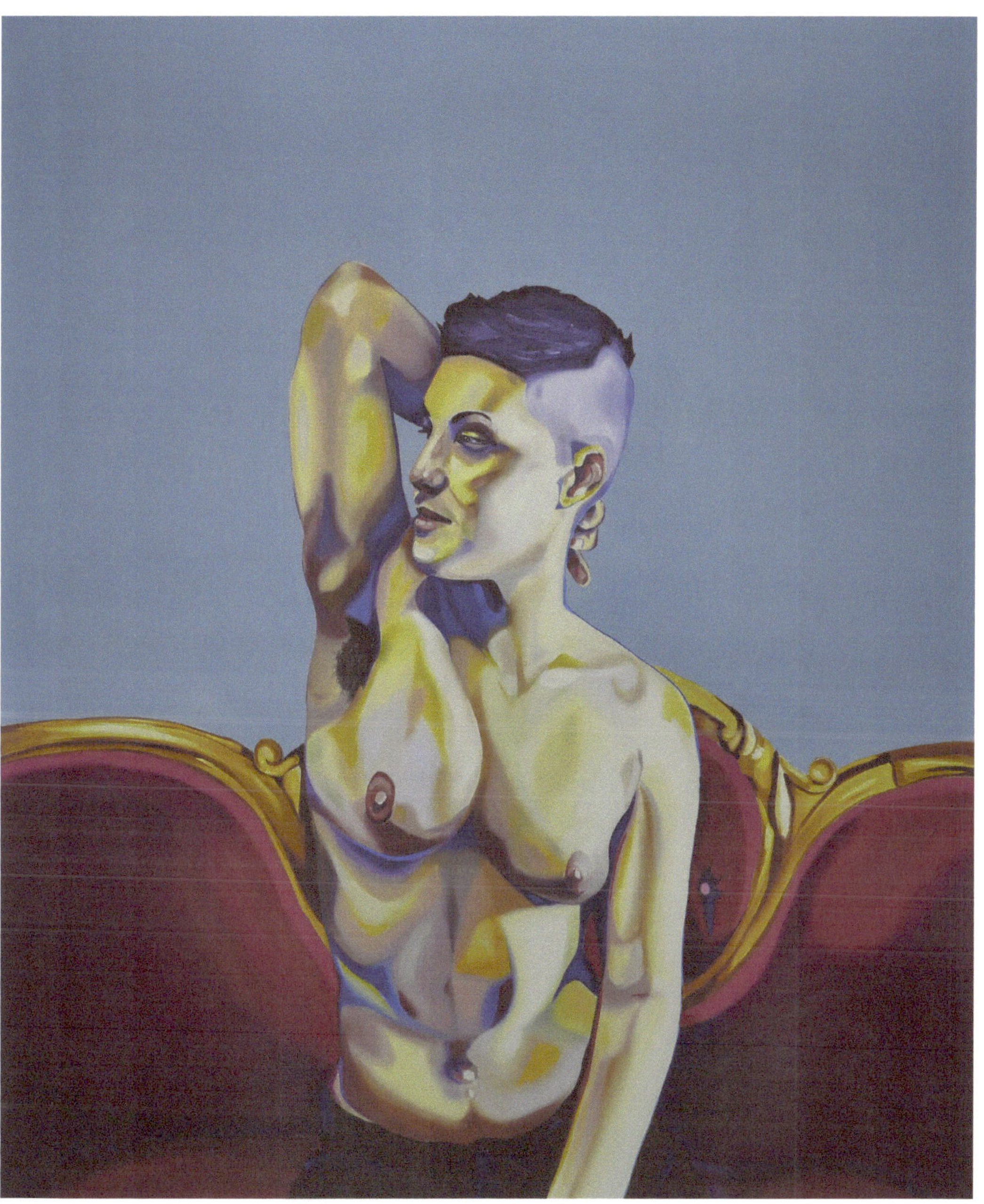

TERRI

I was in the Navy in 1985. It was a witch hunt. I was always scared. I always felt like a girl. My friends, they knew. My dad had a hard time with it at first, but he's over it now. I've had a crazy life. I've never really had any downs, only ups. I was fascinated with showgirls. When I got out of the service in 1989, I didn't want to come back to Kansas City. I hated growing up here. It was so boring. It was, and is, way behind the times. I decided to go to hair school and was doing shows at night. I was building up my name until about 1994, and then all these big names started putting me in their shows. The first time I saw the Ms. Continental Pageant was in 1992. I knew I was different, but I finally figured out I wasn't who I wanted to be. When I saw those girls, I knew that's what I wanted to do. I started my hormones and transitioned from being a drag queen to really being a woman.

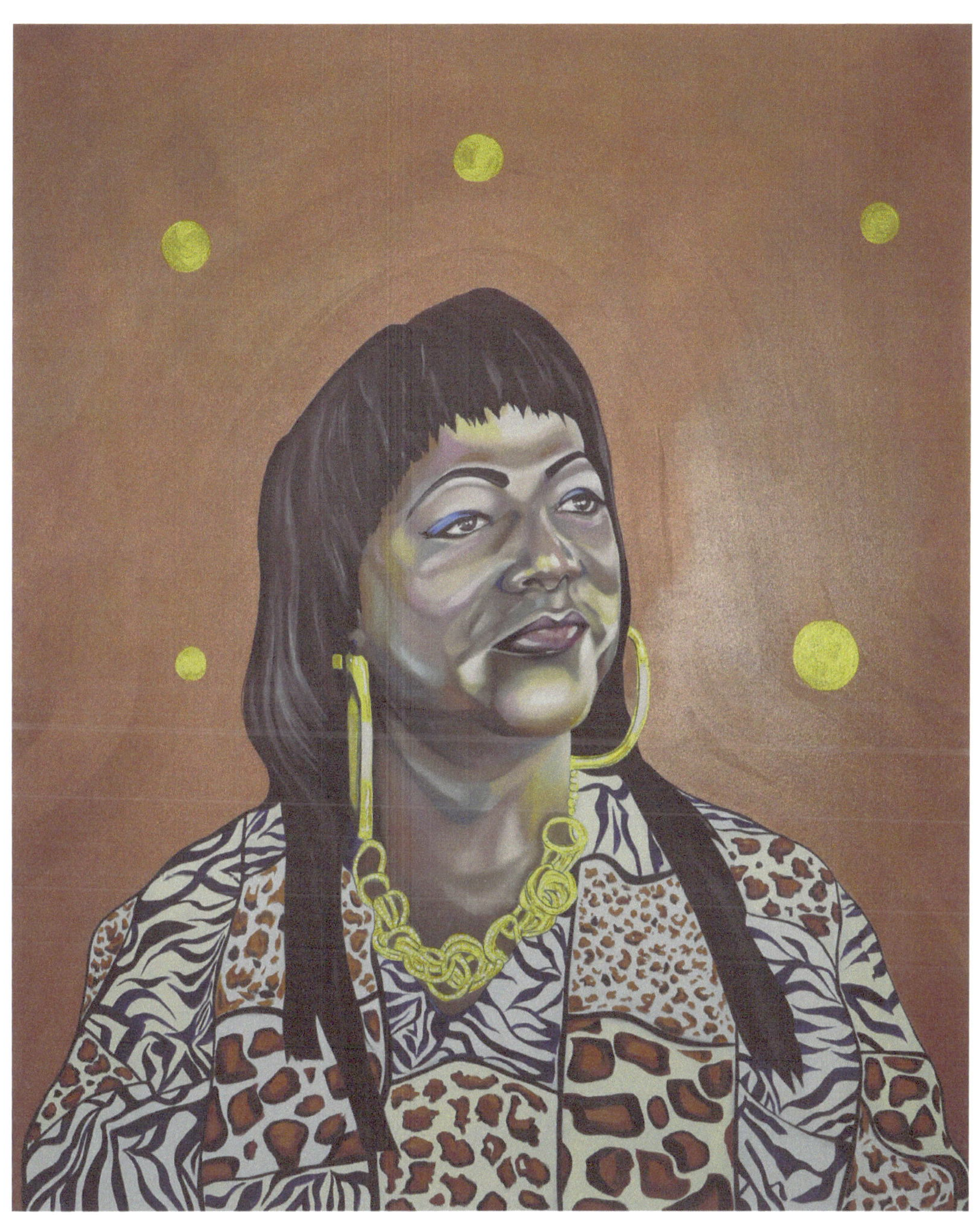

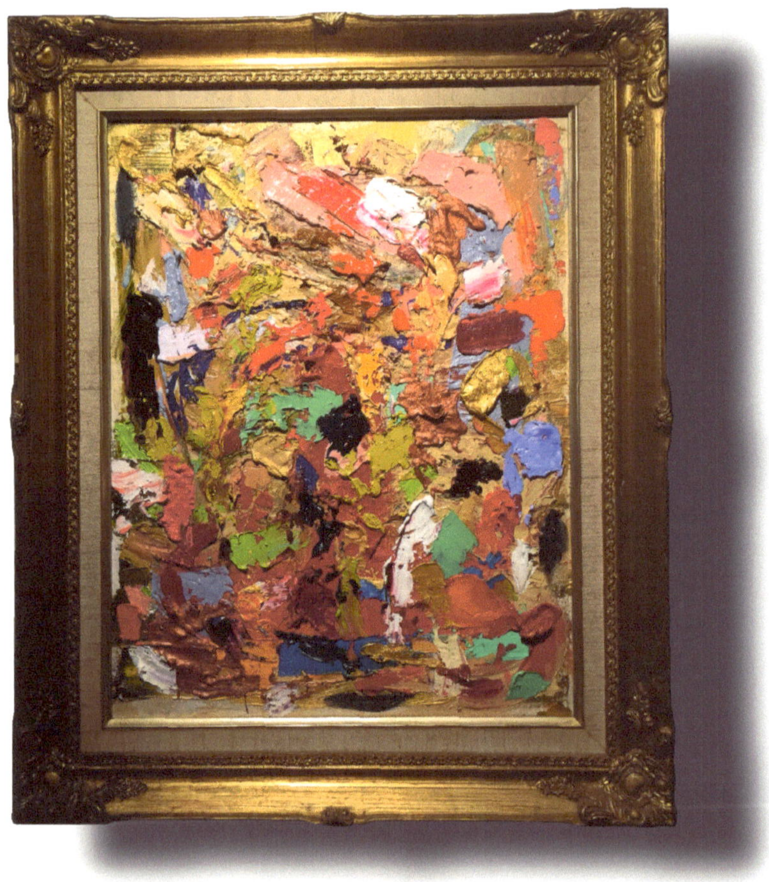

Each time I started a new *Gender Treason* painting, I mixed a fresh pallet full of different skin tones and colors, which spoke directly to the spirit of that subject. When the painting was finished, I used a pallet knife to put what was left over on this framed canvas.

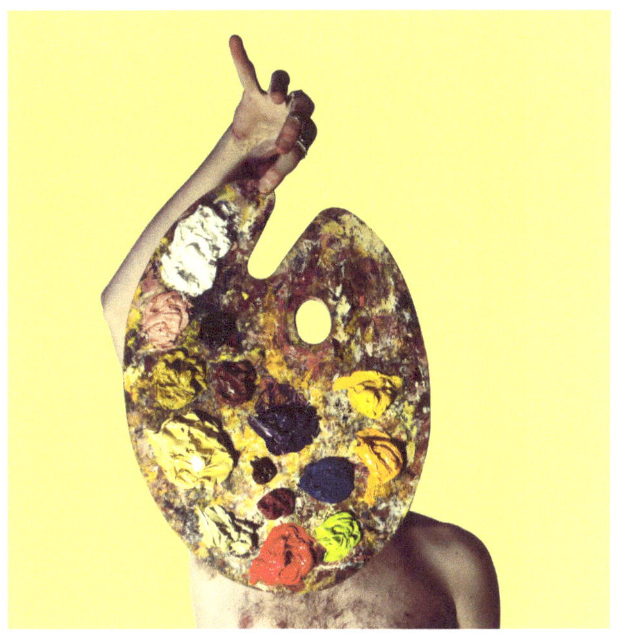

Ryan Wilks is a self-taught artist who works predominantly in the medium of oil paints. Major themes in his work centralize on issues of gender and sexual identity. His use of wild colors (and understanding of tonal value) has been influenced by the works of Paul Gauguin and Wayne Thiebaud. While traveling across the country and cultivating a less conventional education, he has developed working relationships with artists in Chicago, San Francisco, and Kansas City, which helped shape his decision to focus on the expressive and emotional honesty of portraiture.

wilkspainting.com

www.ingramcontent.com/pod-product-compliance
Lightning Source LLC
Chambersburg PA
CBHW042131030726
47599CB00002B/432